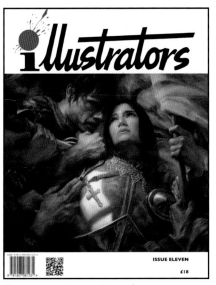

Cover Image: Donato Giancola

Illustrators
The Book Palace
Jubilee House
Bedwardine Road
Crystal Palace
London SE19 3AP

Email: IQ@bookpalace.com
Web: www.bookpalace.com
Contact GW: gw@bookpalace.com
Tel: 020 8768 0022
(From overseas +44 20 8768 0022)
Publisher: Geoff West
Editor & Designer: Peter Richardson
Consultant Editor: David Ashford
Featured Writers: Peter Richardson, Jennifer Gori, David Ashford, Mike Terry
Website: Paul Tanner
Subscriptions & Distribution: David Howarth
Advertising: ads@bookpalace.com

illustrators ISBN 978-1-907081-28-6
ISSN 2052-6520
Issue Number Eleven Published Summer 2015
Copyright © 2015 by The Book Palace Ltd.

illustrators is published quarterly.
Each issue £18
4 issue subscription UK £59
4 issue subscription EU £72
4 Issue subscription USA/ROW £77

Available in the USA from **budplant.com**
Trade Orders: IQ@bookpalace.com
or gazellebookservices.co.uk

Printed in China by Prolong Press Ltd

ISSUE ELEVEN

CONTENTS

EDITORIAL

Donato Giancola is not only one of the premier fantasy artists of the 21st century, but this master artist, craftsman, visionary and winner of enough awards to fill several display cabinets is also an incredibly helpful and unassuming guy. All of which has added to the joy that we experienced when working on bringing you the story of his extraordinary rise to pre-eminence in the realms of fantasy art.

Tomer Hanuka is another artist who has risen to the top of what is a highly competitive and fickle profession. His graceful line, dynamic use of solid black and inspired use of colour, offset by his darkly deviant iconography, has garnered a worldwide fan base and commissions from Jack White to DC Vertigo comics. Jennifer Gori reveals more about Tomer's life work and inspirations.

David Ashford relates the story of James McConnell, one of the "Pulpiest" artists the UK has ever spawned. David's text brings to life a man whose devotion to his art remained a constant throughout his long anf successful career.

Mike Terry's wit, warmth and brilliant caricatures have led to a string of prestigious commissions spanning the world of advertising and, more recently, children's picture books. Mike shares with us some of those memories and brings us up to date with what is currently on his drawing board.

Freya Hartas is the latest young illustrator to be spotlighted in our 'Out There' column. She is already making waves in the field of publishing.

Finally we are sharing one of Jonathan Burton's amazing posters with his unique take on a classic Vincent Price film, 'The House on Haunted Hill'.

Thanks to Mark Terry of *facsimiledustjackets.com* for his restoration of several James McConnell covers and Norman Boyd for all his work on our behalf.

Donato Giancola

Peter Richardson looks at the work of a man whose quest for enlightenment has brought his art to the attention of millions.

DESPITE A LIST OF AWARDS and achievements that would effortlessly gobble up this feature's entire word count, Donato Giancola is a refreshingly grounded and modest guy. He is disarmingly unassuming about a talent and drive that has seen him raise the bar on excellence in the field of fantasy illustration. The knock-on effect of which has been to create a renaissance in the commissioning of fantasy art illustration as well as inspiring a new generation of artists to follow in his wake.

His day starts with preparing his two daughters' packed lunches and cycling off with them to their school. By 9.00 am he is in his Brooklyn studio sorting through the daily deluge of emails from fans and professionals, and then by 10.00 am he is finally ready to launch himself into the intense creative process that goes into generating images that have seared their way into the consciousness of art lovers from around the world.

He reckons on a clear run of five hours before school pick-ups and various other commitments (that include teaching at the New York School of Visual Arts) begin

FACING PAGE LEFT: 'Archer of the Rose', 2008.
FACING PAGE RIGHT: 'Red Sonja, painted in 2007.
ABOVE: 'Shaman's Loss' winner of the Silver Medal from *Spectrum: the Best in Contemporary Fantastic Art* and a finalist in the Figurative category at the *Art Renewal Center*'s 2010 Salon.
RIGHT: Sea-borne tragedy recurs in 'The Wreck of the Whydah' 2014, 96" x 48".

to nibble at his time. As he reflects ruefully, it was not like that when he first entered into the world of illustration in 1993 when he could devote ten hours at a stretch to his painting.

Giancola's artistic odyssey is both fascinating and instructive. He was born Daniel Giancola in 1967 and raised in Colchester, Vermont. From an early age he displayed a passion for drawing {his parents still have art dating back to his First Grade class) and as his interests grew and multiplied he would use his love of drawing as a way of processing the themes that were occupying his attention. His passion for history has been a constant, but growing up in the 1970s he was swept up by *Star Wars* and, science fiction movies, constructing model kits and dioramas, and creating artwork so that every fibre of his being was invested in the world of imaginative adventure. Similarly his love of comics saw him creating new legions of super-powered heroes and when he fell under the spell of role-playing, *Dungeons and Dragons* and *Traveller* provided fuel for the creation of aliens, mages and mystics to inhabit worlds complete with maps for them to navigate within.

At the end of his High School studies, Donato enrolled

FACING PAGE: 'St. George and the Dragon'. Oil on panel, 24" x 30", painted in 2010.
ABOVE: 'The Tower of Cirith Ungol'. Painted in 2012.
BELOW: Gandalf in 'You Cannot Pass', 2007.

at the University of Vermont, intent on pursuing a career in electrical engineering, but was disappointed to discover that there was none of the scientific creativity that he had anticipated. Looking for other modules that he could explore and find satisfaction within, he enrolled on his very first drawing course—receiving his first formal art tuition at the age of 20. The experience proved so rewarding, that the following semester he added painting and art history to his studies. As Donato recounts; "… after a year and a half my art teachers said to me; *you should go somewhere else, you work hard, you're motivated, you should go to an art school where you can be properly challenged.* "

So, taking their advice, Donato eventually landed at Syracuse University and committed himself to a BFA in painting. It was here at Syracuse that Donato found and refined his artistic voice. His extra-

curricular activities included membership in a comics appreciation society that would draw in students from other disciplines. As a result he was creating comics with students studying law and medicine, but all sharing the same passion for worlds outside of the ordinary. Here again, he found himself thoroughly captivated by the challenges of creating virtual worlds but now, with the interaction of artistic peers, he was able to hone, develop, and refine his visions. His commitment to what courses Syracuse could offer was total and, with access to a studio, all of Donato's spare time was invested in creating personal projects in addition to those required to fulfil the demands of the degree. As he observes, "The real way to discover the career potential in someone is to find out what they do outside of the classroom", adding that, "what you do as a hobby is something that is going to define you as a successful professional".

BELOW: 'Lancelot and Guinevere'. 18" x 22", oil on panel 2004.
RIGHT: 'Waiting'. 48" x 36", oil on panel, 2010.
A haunting melancholia informs much of Giancola's work—his brush delineates a world of star-crossed lovers and doomed trysts, set in a sea of foreboding, illumined by faltering sun shafts.

Upon graduation, he decided to move to New York. For him, it was a logical choice as it brought him within the orbit of other artists and most importantly it was where Barracca Associates, an artist representative, was located. Giancola had flagged himself up to both Sal Barracca and his partner art director Joe Curcio at a Syracuse University portfolio review held for graduating students. A follow up interview had taken place at the agency's New York office and, although Sal considered Giancola's work a little too raw to start representing him immediately, he saw great potential. It was under Sal's encouragement that Donato commenced building up a folio of sufficiently professional looking work to attract the attention of Sal's clients, who were primarily New York-based publishers specialising

ABOVE: 'Shaman' 2006. 24" x 36" oil on panel. Giancola's eye for a strong design, coupled with masterly use of lighting, ensure that his paintings draw the viewer in like a moth to a flame.

in science fiction and fantasy—precisely the areas of commercial art Donato had targeted. Working back at his parent's house in Vermont, Donato would spend a month painstakingly working up each sample before making the trek down to New York City to show Sal his latest offering. Sal's reviews were excruciatingly thorough and honest, and Donato would then head back home to make the necessary adjustments as well as to begin working on yet another sample.

It was September 1992 when Donato finally made the move to New York City to commence a more thorough working relationship with Sal. He resisted the temptation to get a 'regular' job and instead supported himself with part-time work at the Society of Illustrators, initially as a coat checker. Donato lived in an apartment he shared

RIGHT: 'Construct of Time'
Cover for the novel 'Shadows
Fall' by Simon Green
published 1993. 18" x 27",
oil on panel.

with two other aspiring artists and in his free time continued to create samples for his portfolio.

Donato credits the move to New York City as one of the wisest in his professional career. His thirst for self-improvement and mastery of his craft was such that he spent hours at art museums such as The Metropolitan Museum of Art, where he fully immersed himself in the work of artists such as Rembrandt, Rubens and Caravaggio, making studies and copies of their works so that he could better understand their procedures. In addition to attendance at life drawing classes he also managed to secure a post as assistant to the noted figure painter Vincent Desiderio. Any free moments were spent at gallery openings where he revelled in the works of major contemporary figurative artists such as Odd Nerdrum. In short his commitment to his career path was utterly focused and he was making all the decisions necessary to put him in pole position to be able to pursue a career as a leading exponent of fantasy art.

His efforts finally paid off, when on a cold grey Monday in December 1992, he received a phone call from Sal with not one, but three covers for a set of classic science fiction novels: *The Time Machine* by H.G. Wells, *A Connecticut Yankee in the Court of King Arthur* by

ABOVE: Another of the early series of book covers that launched Giancola's career, '20,000 Leagues Under the Sea'. "16 x 23", oil on masonite.
ABOVE LEFT: Donato Giancola's first book cover commission, 'A Connecticut Yankee in King Arthur's Court', published in 1993.

ABOVE: The cover for the novel
'Otherness' by David Brin,
published in 1994. Oil on masonite
14" x 30".
ABOVE RIGHT & FACING PAGE:
'Inherit the Earth', Cover
commission for the novel by Brian
Stableford. 34" x 22". Oil on
panel, painted in 1998.

Mark Twain and Jules Verne's, *Journey to the Centre of the Earth.* As Donato says, "I could not have asked for better commissions for initiation into the field of professional illustration!"

Over the intervening years Donato has built up his work within the publishing field, so that he can now look back with great satisfaction, having had the opportunity to illustrate texts which have been a source of inspiration since he was a teenager. Pre-eminent amongst these are his commissions for J.R.R. Tolkien's *The Lord of the Rings.* The first of these came his way in 1995 when he received a call from the art director at Iron Crown Enterprises inviting him to contribute artwork for a Middle-Earth card game that they were due to launch under the title of 'Wizards'. Giancola sent his portfolio over and the art director was so impressed with what he saw that he offered Donato as many cards as he wanted to paint within the time available. Donato initially agreed to fifteen and once those were delivered the client was so captivated that more and more were commissioned for future decks.

It was four years later that the *Science Fiction Book*

ABOVE: Cover for 'Psycho historical Crisis'
by Donald Kingsbury. Painted in 1999,
measuring 36 ''x 22''. Oil on Masonite.
LEFT: Cover for the novel 'Godheads' by
Emily Devenport. Oil on masonite,
15'' x 22'', painted in 1997.
It's interesting to note that Giancola's early
covers opted for a much brighter palette
than his later dark fantasy paintings.

ABOVE: 'Iron Man'. Measuring 36" x 24", this is one of Giancola's comparatively rare super-hero themed creations; painted in 2008, RIGHT: 'Earth to Universe', 1998. This is one of several robotic themed paintings that Giancola has created. Measuring 18" x 20" and painted in oil on panel in 1998.

Club approached him to provide artwork for the cover of a new edition of *The Lord of the Rings*. The resultant artwork brought to the fore Giancola's ability to invest his works with power and poignancy as the wraparound artwork portrays. Desiring to include the three main protagonists in one image, Giancola depicted the scene in Balin's Tomb in Moria. An exhausted Frodo slumps into the arms of Aragorn, his hand reaching out to the ring in the circle of light that falls on his vulnerable throat. Another hand reaches up from the bottom of the painting to grab the ring—but this hand is dark and withered, perhaps the hand of Gollum, or Sauron or even Frodo himself as he succumbs to the power of the ring.

The painting is a masterpiece, and as Giancola reflects, was the launch pad for a large body of work which now constitutes his second stage of narrative picture making. Two years later his painting for the cover of *The Hobbit* set the seal on what he still considers to be the greatest success of his artistic career.

Donato's work gained further prominence when, at the same time as he was creating the card artwork for Iron Crown Enterprises, he was commissioned by Wizards of the Coast to contribute art for their 'Magic: The Gathering' series of collectable cards. The contact came via a colleague of his, the illustrator Byron Wackwitz, who was already working for them and could see that Donato's art would be perfect for their ever expanding

14

ABOVE: 'The Taming of Smeagol'. Oil on panel, 36" x 48", painted in 2008.
LEFT: 'The Hobbit Expulsion' cover for the graphic novel. Oil on panel, 68" x 38".
BOTTOM LEFT: 'Eowyn and the Lord of the Nazgul'. Oil on panel, 39" x 34".
BOTTOM RIGHT: 'The Lord of the Rings', oil on panel, 55" x 33", 1999.
The works of Tolkien are a continuous source of inspiration for the artist.

range of fantasy orientated gaming cards. Giancola sent his portfolio to their art director, Sue Ann Harkey, who promptly commissioned him to produce four cards: "Grinning Totem', 'Amber Prison', 'Village Elder' and 'Moss Diamond' were the first of many paintings that Donato was to produce for this world famous series of cards.

But Giancola's work is not confined to the areas of book publishing and game cards, his work has appeared in titles such as *Playboy*, *National Geographic*, promotional material for *Hasbro* and *Star Wars* as well as commissions for video games, concept designs and The United Nations. His profile received yet another boost when he was commissioned by the U.S. Space Programme to create two stamps to commemorate the astronaut Alan Shepard and the Mercury Mission.

In addition to his published work his income receives a sizeable boost from a growing circle of private commissioners and collectors who are the proud owners of many of his originals. It is partly for this reason, along with his love and commitment to mastering the craft of traditional oil painting, that Giancola continues to eschew the convenience of generating his work digitally. He instead creates all his art by hand and his

Text continues on page 32

Working drawings and the finished artwork for another scene from 'The Lord of the Rings'. Giancola's rendition of 'The Fellowship of the Ring - Descent from Caradhras' is a truly epic production. Measuring 114" x 73" and painted in oil on linen, this staggering artwork now resides in a private collection. Prints of this masterpiece are available from the artist's website.

ABOVE: 'Cartographer: Claudia Rodriguez'. Measuring 22" x 17" and painted in oil on panel, this magnificent image was created for the premier publisher of fantasy trading cards; *Wizards of the Coast* in 2002.

LEFT: Cover art for 'Range of Ghosts' by Elizabeth Bear; published by *Tor Books* and Art Directed by Irene Gallo in 2012. It's worth noting that Irene has long been a champion and mentor to many fantasy artists such as Donato Giancola. BELOW:'Prometheus'. Measuring 77" x 95", this is another gargantuan production. Painted in oil on linen in 2005 this painting is one of several that explore space technology.

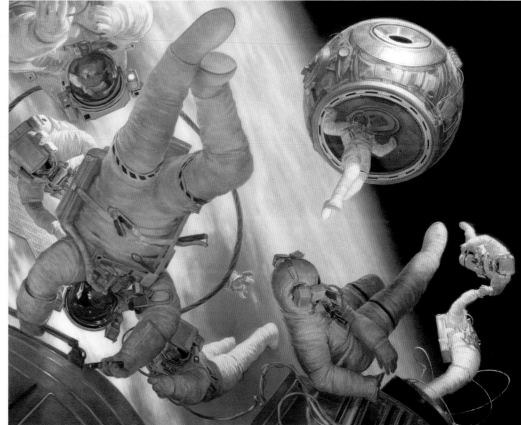

ABOVE: 'Artemis', 2007. A truly captivating display of strong design and sublime use of dappled light. 24" x 36", oil on panel.

RIGHT: 'Night's Watch' for the George R.R. Martin, 2015 *A Song of Ice and Fire* calendar. Featuring portraits of many of the artist's friends and associates, including Martin himself as the figure in the foreground.

FACING PAGE: Another portrayal of 'Red Sonja' in feisty mode, painted in 2009.

Giancola's magnificent 'Joan of Arc'.
Painted in 2012 and measuring
24" x 42", its creation was documented
in a 4 hour DVD available at;
www.donatoart.com/joanofarc/index.htm

The creation of 'Sorrow' from the chalk and graphite concept drawing, through to detailing and the final image, measuring 27" x 33", painted in oil on panel. "Completed in 2014: steeped in classical allusion, the sense of loss it portrays is a theme which Donato frequently revisits in his work.

LEFT: 'Forging the Iron Throne', an image from the 2015 *A Song of Ice and Fire* calendar. The images are based on a series of epic fantasy novels by the American novelist and screenwriter George R. R. Martin.

ABOVE: Another illustration from the 2015 *A Song of Ice and Fire* calendar, 'Tyrion Lannister and Shae'. Giancola's staging and choice of "camera angle" derives as much from his early exposure to comic strips as it does from his understanding of the principles of classical art.

ABOVE: 'Whispers from the Past' was worked up from an image selected by private commissioners from Donato's sketch book. The artist, like many of his contemporaries, has had a long standing fascination with astronauts and this beautiful and poignant painting is the perfect realisation of that passion.

FACING PAGE: Winner of the *Hamilton King Award* by the *Society of Illustrators*, 'The Golden Rose' is another in the artist's compelling series of paintings exploring themes of loss and despair.

RIGHT: The cover painting for 'Kushiel's Dart', the classic novel by Jacqueline Carey, published by the *Science Fiction Book Club* in 2013. BELOW: The artist at work in his Brooklyn studio. Donato's art continues to evolve into new avenues and outlets with a move to producing gallery art as well as his commissions from Art Directors and private patrons, ensuring a constant flow of work.

Text continued from page 17

reliance on digital technology only goes as far as use for post production with print ready files, transfer of preliminary drawings and website promotion. Once he has committed to a finished design from his sketches it goes straight on to panel.

Giancola's work continues to evolve with a move to producing gallery art, where he can explore self generated themes such as his 'Silent Tragedies' show at New York City's *Last Rites Gallery,* and his showing with the *Jean Cocteau Art Gallery* in Santa Fe, which hosted his recent calendar art for George R.R. Martin's *A Song of Ice and Fire* and new science fiction paintings in December and January of 2014—2015. In addition to his teaching duties at the New York School of Visual Arts and the Illustration Master Class, he is now teaching and mentoring students via a series of online lectures on the art and craft of illustration at the SmArt School, sharing his knowledge with a worldwide audience of students.

Donato's artistic efforts have more than paid off in his career: aside from an enviable list of awards including three Gold and six Silver Medals from Spectrum; twenty Chesley Awards from the Association of Science Fiction and Fantasy Artists; three Hugo Awards from the World Science Fiction Society, and the the Hamilton King Award from the Society of Illustrators, his work is now seen by an audience of millions and in the process he has made a huge contribution to the current revival of interest and excitement in the art of illustration.

With his enthusiasm as unquenchable as ever, we have the feeling that the best is yet to come from this remarkable artist. ●

● *For more of Donato's incredible work check out:*
http://www.donatoart.com
He is also contributes to the Muddy Colors blog:
http://www. muddycolors.blogspot.com
For opportunities to learn with Donato through the SmArt School check out:
http://www.smarterartschool.com

James E. McConnell (1903-1995) Original Art

The Battle of Isandlwana 1879

The Battle of Ulundi 1879

IllustrationArtGallery.com

The world's largest gallery of illustration paintings and comic strips

'el: 020 8768 0022 (from outside UK+44 20 8768 0022) E: art@illustrationartgallery.com

Tomer Hanuka

Join Jennifer Gori as she attempts to get under the skin of one of the most challenging, original and inspiring illustrators currently making waves.

LEFT: Tomer's idiosyncratic juxtapositions, bold palette and exquisite draftsmanship are well to the fore in this illustration for 'Life of Pi', which was short-listed in a competition to illustrate the book, **ABOVE:** 'Night Probe' from *American Illustration* magazine, 2006, with its unsettling iconography is a masterly take on the never ending conflicts that assail the Middle East.

FEW ILLUSTRATORS CAN TALK about their involvement with the Oscars, but Tomer Hanuka is one who can. However, it would be over simplistic to reduce one of the most brilliant representatives of contemporary illustration to a simple Hollywood anecdote.

Since his graduation from the New York School of Visual Arts, the Israeli comics illustrator has had an impressive career, collecting some of the most prestigious awards of the profession, such as those from the *Society of Illustrators* and the *Society of Publication Designers*. But,

again, these prizes, for all their undeniable prestige, are not eloquent enough to describe the dynamic style of Tomer Hanuka, with its bold and vivid colours, multi-layered narratives and arresting compositions. Achieving the status of a multi award-winning artist has allowed him to exercise his talent in many directions and fulfil many ambitions.

He who dreamt of illustrating the covers of the *New Yorker* and the *Times* has now fully realised his youthful ambition and is boldly pushing his art into new territory.

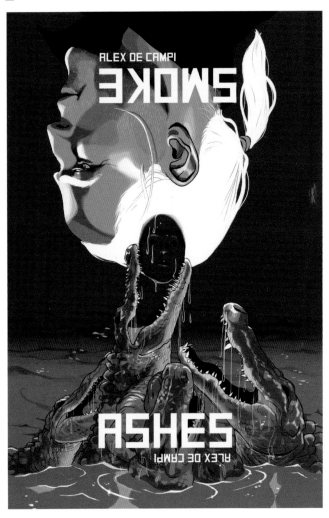

ABOVE: One of a pair of 'flip covers' for Alex De Campi's twin graphic novels, 'Fresh Smoke'.
ABOVE RIGHT: 'Badlands' a print for *Mondo* celebrating the work of Terence Malick. Type design by Avi Neeman
BELOW: 'Iraqi Refugees' 2006.
FACING PAGE: 'The Other Story', cover for *Canongate Books* commissioned in 2006.

"I honestly can't recall having any other plans regarding what I should do as an adult", he admits.

★ ★ ★

Born in 1974, Tomer Hanuka discovered his destiny in Israel, during the economic boom of the 1980s. America was a huge cultural presence no one could escape. The teenager, with his twin brother Asaf, spent his time devouring comics, soaking up the American pop-culture. They were the perfect synthesis of teenagers' fantasies: hyper-saturated, testosterone fuelled and wildly fantastic. The young Tomer readily embraced this universe and made *Marvel Comics*, *Mad Max* and *Ninja Turtles* the basis of his vocation. A vocation shared with his twin, Asaf Hanuka, who is also an illustrator.

"Asaf and I both left Israel in our early 20s. Asaf went to France and studied comics and animation in Lyon, and went on to work for the French comics market. As for me, I packed and moved to New York City, studied illustration at the School of Visual Arts and became an editorial illustrator."

But the Atlantic Ocean could not separate the pair, united both by blood and art. "We are sharing a similar

ASAF HANUKA   TOMER HANUKA   BOAZ LAVIE

the DIVINE

vision but, since we had quite a different type of education and work experience, our combined sensibilities are diverse and complimentary, and hopefully it makes the end result richer."

Tomer and Asaf have thus collaborated in several illustration projects, including comic book 'Bipolar' (*Alternative Comics*, from 2000 to 2004) and graphic novel 'The Divine', co-created with writer Boaz Lavie. By chance, the two heroes of the novel are twin boys, but fighting with more than pencils.

Child soldiers in South East Asia, they team up with an American mercenary who becomes entangled with their mythic struggle against forces of oppression. A very full agenda!

Violence is always intrinsic in the creations of Tomer, scattered with wit, along with non-conformism, irony and eroticism. These themes do not preclude poetry and fantasy, and suggest that much of the innate tension in his work derives from an oscillation between childhood dreams and adult cynicism.

Text continues on page 42

FACING PAGE: The twin brothers who are central to 'The Divine'' appear in this illustration commissioned for *Juxtapoz* magazine.
LEFT: Cover to *Bipolar 1* published by *Five O'Clock Shadow* in 2000.
ABOVE LEFT: 'From God's Mountain IV' Concept art for 'The Divine'.
ABOVE: Cover to 'The Divine' scheduled for publication in July 2015. Written by Boaz Lavie this project is yet another collaboration between the twin brothers Tomer and Asaf.

ABOVE & RIGHT: 'From God's Mountain' pages from 'The Divine'.
FACING PAGE: The tension rises in this page from 'The Divine' with pencils by Asaf and inks and colours by Tomer. Written by the celebrated writer, film maker and game designer Boaz Lavie, 'The Divine' is published by *First Second*, July 2015.

HE BECAME
BLIND. THEN
HE DIED.

I'M ALL
FOR YOU...

BECAUSE
YOU THINK
WE ARE
KIDS

YOU LIKE KIDS,
YOU ARE NOT
AFRAID OF
KIDS.

WELL I
ACTUALLY
___

YOU CAN
HELP US WIN,
OR YOU CAN
STAY HERE.

BUT IF YOU STAY
HERE, WE TAKE OUT
YOUR EYES. BECAUSE
YOU SAW US.

STOP !!!

Text continued from page 39

He is quite cautious when it comes to acknowledging any allusion to humour in his creations. "I'm not sure I have an agenda that is specific in that regard. I try to express the feelings that fit the article or story I'm working through. Hopefully there is a range."

If Tomer Hanuka is talking about himself and his work with a certain humility and timidity, it is perhaps as a result of unleashing his creative freedom and uninhibited imagination in his illustrations, which is his primary means of articulating his thoughts and ideas.

Is this terseness a side effect of an American education and its efficacy? Or is it an Israeli vision of the world? This is difficult to determine, as he maintains an aura of reserve when it comes to analysing his work, which is shaped by many influences. References that include Japanese animation and cinema in general.

Movies are one of his passions, his most noteworthy incursion into this industry was his involvement in the animated movie *Waltz with Bashir*, the 2008 project of Ari Folman which achieved a 2009 Oscar Nomination for Best Foreign Movie. Tomer Hanuka was invited to contribute to a scene (the sequence of the dream) by the

Play Boy

art director David Polonsky. He based his drawings on the storyboards, before the team animated them. A task that he found much more demanding than his casual illustration work.

"I had to relinquish control of every line and colour, hoping that something from the compositions and general colour palettes would be preserved. It was hard to let my work go, but the result was powerful—definitely not something I could have done on my own."

After his brush with the Oscars, he also did some animation related work, mainly for the little screen and advertising, as well as some development for other films. He has enjoyed stretching his innate storytelling ability through a sequence of images: "I really enjoy carving

ABOVE: 'Bankers at the Dawn of Civilization', an illustration for *Playboy* magazine from 2009. Art Director, Rob Wilson. LEFT: Tomer's breathtaking poster for Stanley Kubrick's *A Clockwork Orange*, 2014.

43

out the early visual ideas, imagining and fleshing out a complete world that has a consistent visual vocabulary."

For Tomer Hanuka the main imperative with movies is a strong sequence of images rather than the world of Hollywood promotional hype.

Illustration and movies are making good bedfellows. The art of the film poster has been recently revived, mostly by *Mondo*, a company that acquires the licensing to produce official posters, and assigns them to artists. This has presented Tomer with a great opportunity, appealing to both his movie buff side and his thirst for challenges.

"Films are personal experiences that are shared by the masses, and it is an interesting challenge to come up with a visual that is both representative of the public experience, but also explores a personal relationship with the movie. Many times, I end up creating made-up scenes, visuals that were never shot or presented in the movie but seem to create an interesting dialogue with the themes of the movie." His vision of Hitchcock's masterpiece *Psycho* perfectly illustrates this dictum. Hidden in the dark, the beholder is spying Norman Bates carefully dragging out the body of his victim from the shower, in the almost cosy light of the motel bathroom…

In addition his portfolio includes creative film posters for movies *300*, *Rambo* and … *Teenage Mutant Ninja Turtles*! The circle is complete, yet he is still ambitious: his future projects also include illustrating the entire

ABOVE LEFT: 'No Fare, No Well', the crass and the carnal delineated with Hanuka's unerringly elegant line and sublime use of colour, have ensured regular commissions from *Playboy* magazine, as this 2009 illustration commissioned by Art Director Scott Anderson demonstrates.
ABOVE: A voyeuristic POV adds extra chill to this new take on a poster for the Alfred Hitchcock classic *Psycho*.

ABOVE: 'Old Moab',
another noir tinged and
atmospheric artwork for *Playboy*,
commissioned in 2008 by
Rob Wilson.
RIGHT: *Captain Phillips*, Hanuka's
depiction of a tense moment from
the Tom Hanks film which was
reviewed in the January 2009
edition of the *New Yorker*.

ABOVE: A poster for Stanley Kubrick's *The Shining*, one of an ongoing series of posters the artist is creating based on Kubrick's films. ABOVE RIGHT: Another poster from the Kubrick filmography—this time a surreal juxtaposition from *2001 A Space Odyssey*—creates a tense and unsettling image. Type design by Avi Neeman

Kubrick filmography. "But I guess it's going to take a while!"

★　　　　★　　　　★

Moving to New York, the epicentre of American culture, was a great career move for the 22 year-old Tomer. Although it was tough to start with, his parents made considerable financial sacrifices and Tomer took a job in a factory in Queens to help fund himself through the New York School of Visual Arts. But he remained intensely focused on his career and within six months of graduating he received two prestigious awards from *The Society of Illustrators*.

It was the receipt of these two medals at the end of 2000 that really got him noticed and afforded him the opportunity to win prestigious contracts with brands such as *Nike* and *Microsoft*. He made incursions into the music industry, producing some scintillating work for rocker, Jack White and rapper, Aesop Rock. The respect he won in the profession led to collaborations with prestigious publications such as the *New York Times*, *Der Spiegel*, *Rolling Stone*, *MTV* and even *Playboy*!

His sulphurous illustrations also led him to create the red-hot cover for the *Penguin Classics* edition of 'Philosophy in the Boudoir' by the Marquis de Sade. The publisher gave him virtually a free hand and many of the risqué scenes came through unscathed… "To my surprise, the nipple on the girl on the front cover got through without any problem, but a large black horse standing in a living room on the back cover had to undergo visual sterilization," he told Israeli newspaper *Haaretz*.

Yet, illustrating book covers isn't as straightforward as it may seem.

"When I receive a book cover commission, I do my best to read the book. It makes a huge difference in my ability to distil a visual that can work as a cover. After I've finished reading the text, I'm trying to think if there was a moment that lingers, and maybe investigate the viability of that moment as a metaphor for the larger themes the book is exploring."

For most illustrators, pressure is an unpleasant side issue of freelancing: but definitely not for him!

"Deadlines inspire me! An external limit that is imposed

ABOVE: The front and back cover artwork for *Penguin Classics* edition of the Marquis De Sade's 'Philosophy in the Boudoir', published in 2006. Tomer's inspired use of flat colour and tone draws attention to the Beardsleyesque' line work that adds an extra veneer of eroticism to the tableaux.

to the brain makes it magically come up with something…"

One could be jealous of his philosophy. But who could blame him for preferring to rejoice in the perks offered by his work: constant challenge and intellectual stimulation. " I like to draw new things, research things that were previously unknown to me. For example, I recently got to do a cover for *National Geographic*. It was an amazingly inspiring story: a skinny, life hardened 16-year-old girl entering a cave and falling into a deep pit. A team of divers exploring the submerged cave finds her skull: fast forward 13,000 years. It is the oldest skull ever to be found on the American continent. My job was to recreate this girl at the moment when she entered the cave, thousands of years ago. Based on her skull, she was pretty cute!"

Whether it's reviving our ancestors or other subjects, the work process of Tomer is always the same. It begins with research. Then, he makes a lot of small sketches, before he settles for a few larger sketches. At the end, when he is completely satisfied, he breathes life into the final illustration, 100% digital, using a *Wacom Cintiq* with *Adobe Photoshop*. A combination that seems to hum like a well-oiled piece of machinery. But Tomer is not sheltered from difficulties.

"I've burned out a few times. You got to learn when to

FACING PAGE: 'The Sea Bricks'. Cover for *IL* magazine, Italy 2015.
ABOVE LEFT: The cover art for *National Geographic* featuring the story of the discovery of a 13,000 year old skull of a 16 year old girl living on the prehistoric American continent.
ABOVE: Illustration for a review of the opera, 'The Death of Klinghoffer' published in *The New Yorker* November 2014.

ABOVE TOP LEFT: 'The
Possibility of an Island',
illustration for *Playboy*.
ABOVE TOP RIGHT: 'Perfect
Storm', *The New Yorker* 2014.
The original art was created
three years earlier and based
on a Sam Shephard story.
ABOVE: Another concept art
for 'The Divine'.
FACING PAGE: 'Grim Zone'
Boston magazine 2007.

stop and take a break, and that is something that I learnt the hard way. There is a lot of pressure in the beginning to do well and get established, and it isn't hard to lose balance. The danger with over-working is that it's no longer fun to draw, and it results in average drawings. As freelancers, our biggest job might be to preserve the flame of inspiration."

Until now, Tomer is coping very well. Despite the huge amount of work produced for *Penguin Classics*, *Random House*, *Scholastic*, *Tor*, as well as *Marvel Comics* and *D.C. Comics*, he still has spare time for his personal work. When not supplying narratives for his clients, he focuses on his own stories. His bibliography includes some successes such as 'The Placebo Man' (*Alternative Comics*, 2005) a collection of short comics, and 'Overkill' (*Gingko Press*) in 2011. The personal project he is the most proud of is the aforementioned 'The Divine', with Boaz Lavie and his brother Asaf Hanuka.

"It took us five years to finish. I feel that a lot of things

Text continues on page 58

ABOVE: 'Cell'
Entertainment Weekly
magazine 2006. The
illustration depicts an
excerpt from Stephen
King's novel.

ABOVE TOP: 'Darling', an illustration for a *Blue Q* shopping bag, Art Directed by Mitch Nash 2011.
ABOVE: Limited edition print for Tomer Hanuka's monograph 'Overkill - The Art of Tomer Hanuka', published by *Gingko Press*. A signed copy of the print also accompanied the limited edition of the book.

ABOVE: Cover for 'The Gigolo Murder', *Penguin Books* 2006. Art Director Roseanne Serra.
FACING PAGE: *Rambo First Blood: Part 2*, limited edition silk screen print, for *Mondo*.

SYLVESTER STALLONE

MARIO KASSAR and ANDREW VAJNA PRESENT
"RAMBO/ FIRST BLOOD PART II" RICHARD CRENNA
CHARLES NAPIER · STEVEN BERKOFF MUSIC BY JERRY GOLDSMITH EXECUTIVE PRODUCERS MARIO KASSAR and ANDREW VAJNA
SCREENPLAY BY SYLVESTER STALLONE and JAMES CAMERON STORY BY KEVIN JARRE BASED ON CHARACTERS CREATED BY DAVID MORRELL
PRODUCED BY BUZZ FEITSHANS DIRECTED BY GEORGE P. COSMATOS READ THE JOVE PAPERBACK FILMED IN PANAVISION®

R RESTRICTED
UNDER 17 REQUIRES ACCOMPANYING
DOLBY STEREO
IN SELECTED THEATRES
STUDIOCANAL

ABOVE: 'Hyena', a cover for 'Food Chain', published in 2006 by *Canongate Books*.
LEFT: 'Inside Out', an illustration for *Top Shelf*, 2001.
FAR LEFT: Cover for *Penguin Book*'s edition of 'The Kiss Murder' published in 2008.

FACING PAGE: 'Jaw Breaker', *Unmen* No. 7, *DC/ Vertigo* 2007. His elegant line work, exquisite draughtsmanship and dynamic use of colour heighten the shock value of artworks such as this.

ABOVE: Tomer Hanuka in his New York studio, photographed by Michal Rubin.
ABOVE TOP: Hanuka's take on the Hitchcock film, 'Vertigo'.
ABOVE TOP RIGHT: 'Father: Encounter on Dagobah' The Alamo Drafthouse Theatre.

Text continued from page 50

I've picked up during my work in editorial illustration for a decade and a half ended up in the pages of 'The Divine', mostly related to the use of colours, to establish certain focal points in the narrative, or direct the emotional tone."

Now, two decades later, the twin illustrators and brothers Tomer and Asaf are back in Israel and working both apart and together. The successful team of 'The Divine' are now ready for a new adventure. They are working on a new graphic novel, which is, at the moment deep in its research stage.

★   ★   ★

Illustration is a mode of expression for many artists, as well as a way of life, allowing them to achieve their childhood and teenage dreams and to keep a bond with what matters the most to them. Tomer Hanuka has chosen this path and his profession has warmly reacted to his commitment. But beyond recognition and a prolific career, he has succeeded in creating his very own visual identity and impact on contemporary illustration. "A lot of pressure for the future?" No, just one more tall order… ●

● *For more of Tomer's electrifying artwork check out his website , which includes publication details of his works:* **http://thanuka.com/**

IN THE NEXT ISSUE

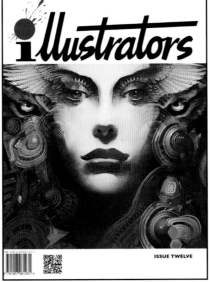

ISSUE TWELVE

Join us as we enter the multi-faceted worlds of Android Jones, as we explore the life and career of this extraordinary creator, whose near death experiences have shaped and driven his art.

Plus the weird worlds of Sidney Sime, the uncensored Howard Chaykin, Denis Zilber's surreal 'toons and Arty Freeman's off-the-wall art.

Sidney Sime

Howard Chaykin

Denis Zilber

Courtesy of the Illustration Art Gallery

ABOVE LEFT: Classic McConnell painting from the cover to 'The Seven Men at Mimbras Springs', published by *Corgi Books* 1960. Ever the pragmatist, McConnell has added the crest of a stetson behind the main figure's right shoulder and the rim of another behind the left arm to fulfil the Art Director's brief.

James McConnell

David Ashford examines the work of an artist whose work brought a spicy US pulp ruggedness to the covers of UK publishing

IF THERE IS ONE BRITISH book cover artist who can convincingly be compared with the best of the American pulp illustrators of the 1940s and '50s, it is James E. McConnell. Together with his near contemporary, Denis McLoughlin (see *illustrators 1* and *The Art of Denis McLoughlin*), McConnell was one of this country's most prolific book cover artists. However, whereas McLoughlin worked almost exclusively for one publisher, *T. V. Boardman*, McConnell seemed to work for practically every book publisher in the U.K. Certainly James E. McConnell could be said to be one of Britain's most ubiquitous and successful book cover artists of all time.

James Edwin McConnell was born in Newcastle-Upon-Tyne, on 15 July 1901. From an early age he loved drawing and exhibited a strong visual

imagination. On leaving school young James worked for a local printers as a blockmaker until he managed to gain a place in the prestigious St. Martin's School of Art in London. Here, he studied part-time, whilst still working in the same trade as a blockmaker. St. Martin's taught him solid draftsmanship, the understanding of anatomy and the intricacies of painting in watercolour: all attributes that were to stand him in good stead for his future career.

On leaving St. Martin's, McConnell was intent on earning a living as an illustrator. By 1933 he had been taken on by the Partridge Agency, one of the foremost illustrators' agents in the country, and was soon producing advertising art and, more importantly, paintings for book jackets. By the end of the '30s he had produced jackets for novels published by such illustrious names in the book

ABOVE: A very early original painting, from an unidentified magazine, brings together all the strengths of a classic McConnell image, the atmospheric lighting heightening the tension between the three protagonists. The influence of US pulp artists such as Norman Saunders is readily discernible.

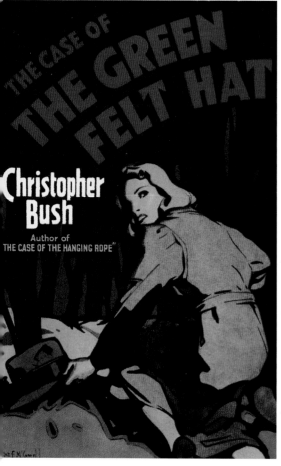

ABOVE: Two of McConnell's covers for *Cassell*'s crime novels. Working within the constraints of cheap commercial printing in the late 1930s, the covers utilise strong dark shapes and bold, bright colours to grab the buyer's attention. FACING PAGE: Despite the more painterly technique, the cover for *Collins* publications, 'Murder in the Coal Hole', still limits its palette to strong oranges interplayed against the black elements of the cellar.

trade as *Collins, Cassell, Faber & Faber* and *Hodder & Stoughton*. These novels were invariably of either the Western or Crime genre.

His early illustrative work exhibits a definite sense of experimentation. Two of the covers he produced for Christopher Bush's Crime novels, published by *Cassell* in the late '30s, illustrate this particularly well. His painting for 'The Case of the Green Felt Hat' is an atmospheric night scene set in a wood in which a young woman is pictured warily picking up the hat of the title. The image is highly reminiscent of contemporary railway posters with the paint laid on in large patches of colour. The other cover, for 'The Case of the Leaning Man', is again set at night with a similar sense of unease but this time it is executed in a loose, painterly style using mostly blue tones with small touches of yellow. A figure is leaning against a lamp post, which is the light source for the picture, while the shadowy figure of a policeman can be seen in the background.

The light source was very important to McConnell. In 'Murder in the Coal Hole', another of his early covers, this time for the publisher Collins, he uses a coal fire as the source, as two figures (one murderously hovering behind the other) lean over towards the viewer, each rendered in subtle tones of

MURDER IN THE COAL HOLE

MILES BURTON

SIGN OF A GOOD DETECTIVE NOVEL

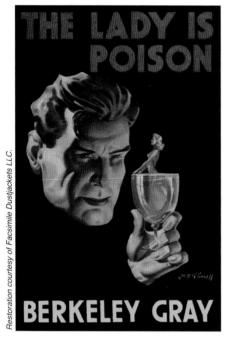

THE LADY IS POISON

BERKELEY GRAY

Restoration courtesy of Facsimile Dustjackets LLC.

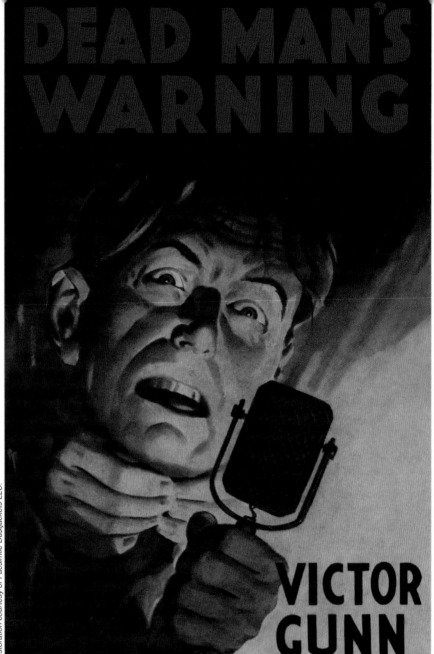

DEAD MAN'S WARNING

VICTOR GUNN

Restoration courtesy of Facsimile Dustjackets LLC.

ABOVE & RIGHT: McConnell's love and mastery of US pulp art came to the fore in the covers he produced for the *Collins Detective and Mystery* series of novels.

FACING PAGE: More of McConnell's Crime novel covers—the more generous spine width of hardbound novels allowed the artist to have two shots at encapsulating the flavour of a story within one image and the spines of McConnell's covers made great use of the opportunity. The spines of these books, when seen in a row, create a wonderful gallery of dramatic and punchy images coupled with bold, punchy lettering.

red. For *Collins* 'Dead Man's Warning', he presents us with a strong close-up of a wide-eyed broadcaster at the microphone, deadly hands clasping his throat. The image is painted in tones of red and brown with the light source throwing a pale yellow hue over his face and the hands. All the crime novel wrappers McConnell designed for *Collins* exhibit the importance of lighting effects in illustration. As he said, "I always concentrated on getting the tones right, light and dark".

During the latter part of the '30s, *Faber & Faber* had recognised his talents and commissioned him to design dust wrappers for their Detective Story compilations; and yet another top publisher, *Hodder & Stoughton*, began commissioning him to paint covers for their Western series. His Western work for *Hodder* was more conventional than his more experimental work on the Crime novel covers but they were nevertheless forceful, produced in a vivid, painterly style.

McConnell found himself extremely busy all through the 1940s, producing dust wrapper illustrations for many titles in the *Collins Detective and Mystery* series of novels, including those featuring the characters, *Chief Inspector Bill*

"Ironsides" Cromwell and the adventurer, 'Norman Conquest'. McConnell was, in fact, Collins' dust wrapper artist of choice for their many Detective novels for almost twenty years and it is not difficult to see why. Although not displaying the powerful sense of design and feeling for the unusual angle that was the forte of Denis McLoughlin, McConnell more than made up for it by his ability to convey menace through the use of colour and lighting effects. Like McLoughlin, he occasionally added symbolic motifs, as for the wrapper design for the 'Norman Conquest' novel, 'The Lady is Poison', in which he portrays a disembodied man's face and a hand holding a wine glass containing a tiny blonde female. It must be admitted, however, that symbolism was not McConnell's strong point.

He was still experimenting and one has only to look at two of his covers for *Collins Wild West Club*, which he produced shortly after the War, to recognise how seriously he was still trying out different techniques. For 'Outlaws of Ophir Creek', he uses sketchy outlines done in coloured chalks to convey the dynamics of a gun duel while, for 'Riders in the Rain', the watercolour paint is applied in such a way that the whole painting appears, most appropriately,

WEST of
WICHITA

Rex
Whitechurch

A FIVE POINT
WESTERN NOVEL

WEST of WICHITA

REX WHITECHURCH

Boardman

OUTLAWS of OPHIR CREEK

RANGER LEE

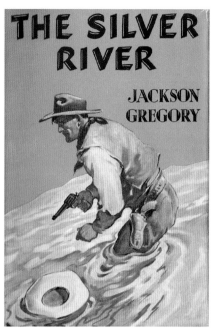

to be drenched in water. There is no doubt that McConnell loved his work and never felt that illustration was a lesser form of art. Late in life he wrote: "I never felt that my work was so commercial that it was just a job. I enjoyed every moment of painting. It was and still is art to me".

With the cheaper end of the book market constantly expanding at the beginning of the 1950s, McConnell found himself increasingly in demand, especially for Crime and Western subjects. At this time there was a surge of interest among the British youth for stories about the Wild West, fuelled by the enormous number of Western films being shown in the cinemas, and McConnell found himself contributing to a variety of Western books geared for the more juvenile end of the market. The publishers, *Birn Brothers*, decided that McConnell was just the man to paint both the covers and the frontispieces for their new series of children's volumes devoted to tales of the Western Frontier, simply called the 'Wild West Book'. *Collins* commissioned him to paint the cover for their 'Bumper Cowboy Book' and the *Children's Press* the cover for a novel for younger readers entitled 'The X Bar X Ranch'. *Juvenile Productions* chose him to paint the frontispieces and no less than five colour plates for their *Riders of the Range* annuals. And it was not only for Western subjects that he found himself in demand. *Thames Publishing* used him for boys' books such as 'Triumphs of Sport and Speed' as well as

ABOVE & FACING PAGE: Like many of the US artists, whose work was a source of inspiration to McConnell, much of his greatest work was produced in response to briefs that demanded dynamic and atmospheric depictions of the Wild West, as these covers for *Collins Wild West Book Club* and *TV Boardman* demonstrate.

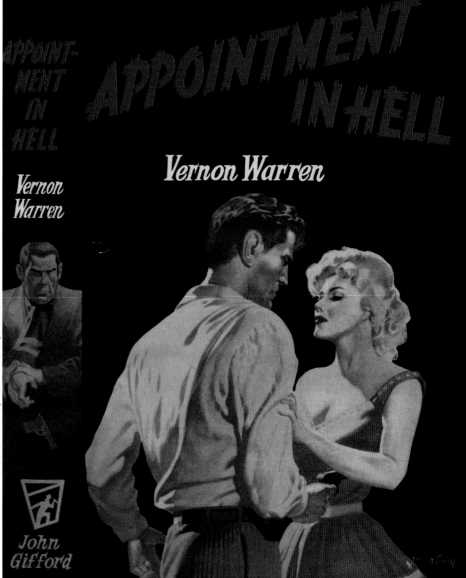

Restoration courtesy of Facsimile Dustjackets LLC.

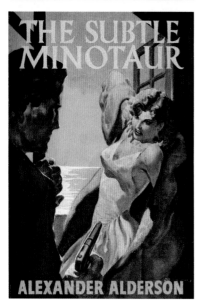

ABOVE: A selection of Vernon Warren titles for _John Gifford_, who made great use of McConnell's command of US styled, "gunzels and molls". Many of these stories were later reissued by the _Thriller Book Club_. 'The Subtle Minotaur' was published in 1954.

girls' stories, such as Phyllis Briggs' 'The Secret Garden'. For their _Kingston Library_ series featuring W.E. Johns' famous Air Ace, _Biggles, Thames_ used McConnell to paint both the dust wrappers and the frontispieces.

In 1950 McConnell had been snapped up by the _Amalgamated Press_ to paint covers for their pocket-sized series of text stories, _The Western Library_. It was for this series he was to produce some of his most lively and vital Western studies, although it must be admitted he also contributed some of his weakest work to the publication as well. There was obviously a time element at play here. It is almost impossible to understand how an artist could keep up such a high standard when taking on such a vast amount of work from so many different publishers. Amalgamated Press editor Leonard Matthews was astounded at McConnell's work rate. As he put it: "McConnell would complete a painting <u>and</u> the rough for the next one, in a day!" Matthews used him for covers for the _A P_'s pocket-sized comics as well, and McConnell found himself contributing not only Western covers for the _Cowboy Comics Library,_ but also historical covers for the _Thriller Comics Library,_ and detective covers for the series of 'Rip Kirby' U. S. reprints published in the _Super Detective Library._

McConnell had, even by the late '40s, been illustrating for Denis McLoughlin's publisher, _T V Boardman_, and was creating all the covers for their Western series of paperbacks. (McLoughlin himself was an admirer

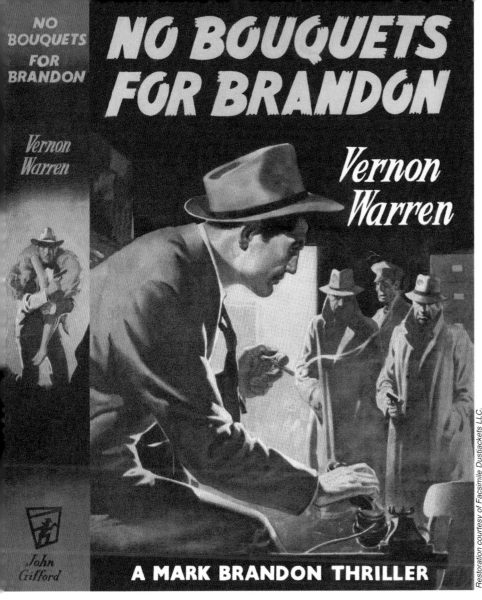

NO BOUQUETS FOR BRANDON

Vernon Warren

A MARK BRANDON THRILLER

John Gifford

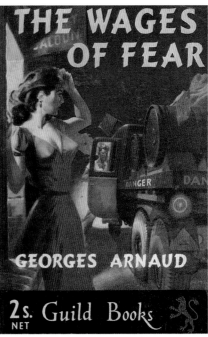

THE WAGES OF FEAR

GEORGES ARNAUD

2s. Guild Books
NET

The Mystery of Dr Fu-Manchu

Sax Rohmer

2s. Guild Books
NET

ABOVE: Covers for paperback publisher Guild Books, featuring 'The Wages of Fear', which became a cult classic when George Clouzot transformed the text into one of cinema's classic "film noirs" and 'Fu Manchu', who was also familiar to generations of moviegoers.

of McConnell's work, particularly for his mastery of the human figure.) In the early '50s, when the *Boardman* imprint changed to that of *The Popular Press*, McConnell began to produce some dynamic covers for their Western pulps. In fact, it could be said that McConnell contributed some of his most vibrant Western work for *Boardman*. His dust wrappers for their series of hardbound Westerns show him at his most sketchy and painterly, as if he was working without restraint, exploring how best to create a feeling of action-packed movement with the minimum of detailed 'finish'.

McConnell was phenomenally busy during the 1950s. In fact, he was now so much in demand by so many publishers for work in so many genres that, in 1953, he felt he no longer needed an agent and he bade farewell to the Partridge Agency.

For the paperback series of thrillers published by *Guild Books*, McConnell was painting covers for Mystery and Crime novels ranging from Georges Arnaud's 'The Wages of Fear' through to Sax Rohmer's 'The Curse of Fu Manchu'. It is fascinating to compare a McConnell Guild cover such as that for 'No Peace for Archer', which is dark and brooding and infused with an atmosphere of malignant evil, with another cover for the same publisher, 'Death in Deep Green', which appears to be painted in sunlight, albeit the necessary sense of menace being still tangible. McConnell showed his versatility by painting covers for no less than twelve of Edgar Rice Burrough's

OPERATION CONQUEST

BERKELEY GRAY

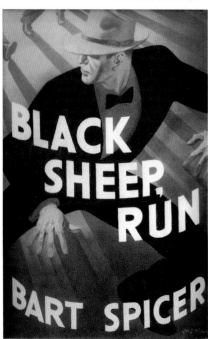

BLACK SHEEP RUN

BART SPICER

ABOVE: The work for *Collins* continued well into the 1950s, while in the field of paperbacks McConnell added new clients such as *Pan Books* to his busy schedule.

GREAT PAN

THE BLUNDERER
Patricia Highsmith

As gripping as a man-trap

Tarzan novels, published as a series of paperback editions by *Pinnacle Books*, although these appear to have been very much a 'rush job' with little thought going into either the design or the execution.

Collins was still using him for their hardback crime novels and, during the '50s, McConnell began to explore more fully new methods of design to evoke the requisite sense of drama and menace. His cover for 'Operation Conquest' is particularly stunning with its use of criss-cross torch beams as the sole source of light as they illuminate a man, his hands raised in the air, black silhouettes of guns pointing towards him in graphic close-up. McConnell combined a powerful blend of realism and pure design in his cover for 'Black Sheep, Run', while his cover for 'Conquest in Scotland' is no less effective with its straight-forward image of a cocksure character with

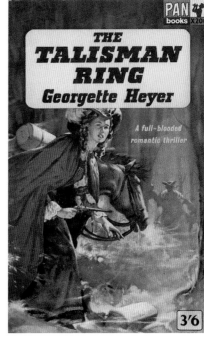

ABOVE: McConnell's work for *Pan Books* included covers for the then popular romantic novelist Georgette Heyer, whose work provided an ideal platform for the artist's command of costumed figurework.

ABOVE & FACING PAGE: The work that McConnell created for *Corgi Books* saw him re-exploring the Western themes which had characterised so much of his work in the previous decades.

a cigarette in one hand and an automatic in the other, which he is pointing straight at the viewer. All three paintings show a maturity of style as well as a sense of an artist attempting to explore the limitations of the crime genre in cover art.

Apart from his painting skills, McConnell's great strength was his mastery of the human figure and it is this that is displayed at its best in his paperback covers for *Pan* and *Corgi*. From the late 1950s and right through the following decade, McConnell was the top cover artist for the popular paperback market. There were few genres that he didn't tackle in his cover work. For *Pan* he contributed a number of covers for historical romances ranging from Lew Wallace's 'Ben Hur' (for which he painted a splendidly lifelike portrait of Charlton Heston) and Rafael Sabatini's 'Scaramouche' to the Regency Romances of Georgette Heyer For the latter series McConnell proved himself to be particularly adept at popularising the Regency period for a modern 1960s audience, admirably interpreting the author's romantic world.

For most admirers of McConnell's work, the paperback covers that show him at his best are the Westerns that he painted for *Corgi Books*. From the late 1950s to the early '60s the covers he contributed to the *Corgi* Westerns were among his finest work. His cover painting for Conrad Richter's 'Sea of

TRAIL SMOKE

Ernest Haycox

He pushed sheep onto the range—and faced death from the gun of every cattleman in the valley!

2'6

Courtesy of the Illustration Art Gallery

ABOVE & FACING PAGE: McConnell's mastery of lighting is well to the fore in these covers for *Corgi Books Western* series. Note the use of both cool and warm reflected light on the skin of the dominant figure on the facing page.
BELOW: McConnell and his faithful Corgi taking in the view at his home in Bookham Surrey.

Courtesy of the Illustration Art Gallery

Grass' exhibits his ability as a pure water colourist, as he evokes the vastness of the landscape by placing the emphasis on the wide-open sky and a subtle treatment of cloud formation. Another cover, for Lee Leighton's 'Lawman', is completely different in approach, emphasising his abilities as a painter of the human form. There is a tremendous vitality about McConnell's western work. His horses in particular, whether simply standing still or galloping hell for leather, are always pulsing with life. However, if there is one single quality that unites all his *Corgi* Western covers, it is McConnell's mastery of light and shade. As he has said: "I love sunlight. The older I get, the more I love it. I always try to put sunlight in my paintings". This passion is very much to the fore in these covers.

In 1976, the then Art Director of *Corgi Books*, John Munday, came across piles of McConnell's original artwork for his Western covers in the *Corgi* Archive and, later that year, eighty of these paintings were exhibited at The Association of Illustrators Gallery in London.

Approaching retirement, he at last began to slow down and by the mid 1960s few book covers could be found illustrated by McConnell. However, like many a fellow contemporary illustrator, he began to contribute to the quality children's educational weekly magazine, *Look and Learn*. He enjoyed working for this magazine as it enabled him to paint covers for every conceivable historical subject and this enjoyment shines through on so

Courtesy of Look and Learn and the Illustration Art Gallery

ABOVE: A superb example of McConnell's later work, which shows no diminution of his enthusiasm for rugged landscapes, magnificent horses and he-man adventure. This cover to the children's weekly *Look and Learn*, which hosted so much of his work, appeared in October 1963.

many of the covers he produced for this magazine.

McConnell finally retired at the age of 73, living with his wife and their Corgi dog in Great Bookham, Surrey, painting landscapes and animal portraits for friends. He lived for very nearly another twenty years, dying in 1995, shortly before his 92nd birthday. McConnell's legacy of artwork was huge: covers for book jackets, paperbacks, magazines and annuals as well as countless frontispieces and colour plates, all signed with his strikingly stylish signature. There are very few illustrators who can begin to equal the sheer variety and quantity of his work and few who can equal the mastery of his painting technique and the dynamism and force of the best of his output. ●

● *I would like to thank my friend, Jim Kealy, who has helped me so much with this project and given me complete access to his impressive collection of McConnell's illustrated books. Without Jim's help this article could not have been written.* **illustrationartgallery.com** *has a large selection of original James E McConnell art for sale.*

DO YOU DARE ENTER?
HOUSE ON HAUNTED HILL

starring **VINCENT PRICE**
CAROL OHMART · RICHARD LONG · ALAN MARSHAL
Produced and Directed by **WILLIAM CASTLE** · Written by **ROBB WHITE** · AN ALLIED ARTISTS PICTURE

ART NOIR:
Jonathan Burton's deliciously wry and beautifully crafted art has been delighting audiences and art directors for over a decade. His achievements include Gold and Silver Medals from *The Society of Illustrators* in New York and Overall Winner of the *Association of Illustrators* in 2013. Jonathan's work will feature in an upcoming issue of *illustrators*, in the meantime here is his take on *House on Haunted Hill* starring Vincent Price. The *Mondo* edition of 350 prints sold out within an hour of its release but there are a limited number of artist's proofs available from Jonathan's site at:

jonathanburton.bigcartel.com

Jonathan's website is at:

jonathanburton.net

The Studio: Mike Terry

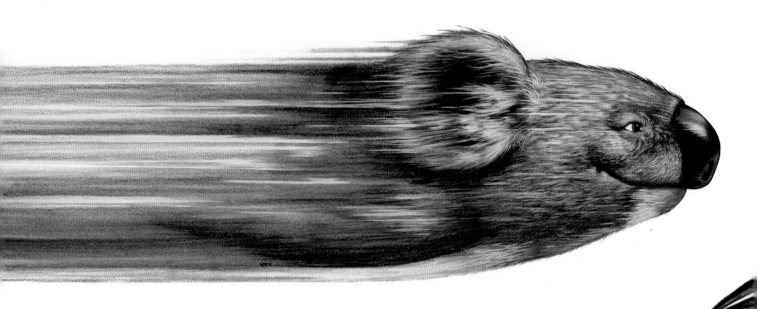

Mike Terry's fun filled caricatures dominated the world of UK advertising throughout the 1970s, garnering awards and acclaim for his ability to add pep and pizazz to whatever campaign he applied his talents to. Beyond that he has carved out a career in children's books and is now applying his talents to fine art and sculpture as he reveals in this Q&A.

PR: Did you always draw?

MT: I was first introduced into the art world, unknowingly at the time, by the head master at junior school, I was asked to write the Lord's Prayer on velum with illuminations. Nearly sixty years later it may well still be there.

My ability grew at senior school resulting in my decision to enter art school at the age of sixteen after staying on for another year to improve my academic subjects due to being dyslexic.

Also, I will always be grateful to two of the teachers there, one of them the art teacher, who put in a good word for me.

And of course my mother and brother who assisted me through art school when I could have been out contributing to a single parent family.

PR: Were any other members of your family artistic?

MT: My mother would write short stories for herself,

ABOVE: Koala for an advert for *Qantas* airlines late 1980s.
LEFT: This brilliant depiction of a teacher for an insurance ad in the 1980s, shows Terry's mastery of caricature which is admirably complimented by his skill as a painter.
FACING PAGE: A painting for the artist's very own letterhead captures the zany pizazz of Mike Terry's art.

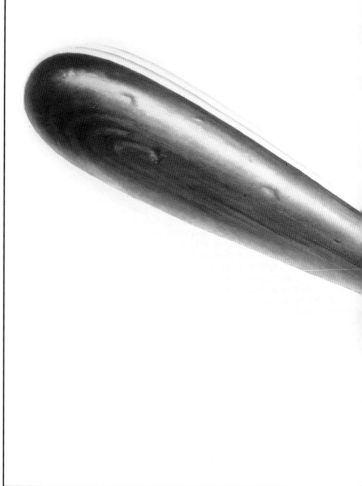

ABOVE: The cover art for Spike Milligan's 'Monty—My Part in his Victory', published 1978 by *Penguin Books*.
ABOVE RIGHT & FACING PAGE: Labour Party Leader, Michael Foot, appearing as Mr. Punch from an illustration for an unused Conservative poster from the 1987 general election.

my elder brother has a talent for drawing and there is someone on my mother's side, the Ormeshers, who was an art teacher.

PR: Where did you train?

MT: I trained at Folkstone Art College from 1964 to '67. Attending art college was transforming, I went from struggling through school because of my handicap, to fulfilling my potential in art.

At that time there were various courses in graphics, fine art, fashion, painting and decorating.

The course I took was Graphic Design and Illustration; we had a couple of full time tutors and freelancers who brought in the outside world.

It was the most transformational three years of my life.

I was sixteen when I started and left when I was nineteen, and was offered a job as a designer in a design department of an office equipment firm off Tottenham Court Road in London, based on my work at the college.

I moved to Muswell Hill, North London and shared a flat with fellow art students from my old art school,—fresh out into the world of work and art and the '60s!

PR: What were your first influences?

MT: The first influence was at senior school. Occasionally we would have an afternoon when students would talk

about their hobbies. A boy in my year talked about bird watching and this appealed to me. This has become a lifelong interest and also a great part in my illustration work for children's books, which usually feature animals.

Then in late 1969 when I was working for a design group as a typographer in London I came across the work of the illustrator Alan Aldridge. At this time this was new and very exciting to see illustration like this used in a magazine.

Alan Aldridge embodied the spirit of the 1960s and for a freshman like me it was the impact of his work with graphic design, bold colours, and faux naïve images. Gone were the days of sombre tones and drabness and in came the evocative psychedelic images.

PR: Did drawing come easily to you?
MT: Drawing was very easy. It was natural to me and was such an enjoyable pursuit. I could use my imagination, capturing the things I found interesting.

PR: Did you find it difficult to break into illustration?
MT: Not at the time. This was the beginning of the 1970s. It was not difficult, it was challenging, a case of being persistent with great dedication, and belief in myself and my work.

I was given a great boost in my career during 1971 in the shape of adverts promoting the company I was

ABOVE: A *Batchelor's Soup* **poster from the 1980s. High profile ad posters, such as this, made a huge boost to an illustrator's earnings. LEFT: UK TV host, Bruce Forsyth.**

ABOVE: 'Think What a Difference a Flower Makes', Quasimodo for *Interflora* advertisement.
ABOVE TOP: Clint Eastwood and Norman Mailer, *Observer* 1980s.
RIGHT: 'People Who Don't Like Football', from another ad campaign.

working for (DPM), a design group, before going freelance. I illustrated these ads and they appeared in an advertising trade publication called *Campaign,* giving me great exposure: later the ads with my illustrations were selected for *Design and Art Direction 72* annual.

PR: What sort of work did you do to begin with?

MT: I was a graphic designer, later moving into typography, working at various design groups and agencies.

By the time I was twenty two and just married I was thinking about moving into illustration. I was inspired by Alan Aldridge, the illustrator, whilst working with the design group *Bowdens* in Soho. It was there that I met Brian Grimwood who was a designer at the time and later to become an illustrator. We have remained friends ever since. He was significant in my development as an illustrator.

From there I moved to working with an agency called *Garland and Compton* to work as a typographer on film

publicity (posters and ads). Whilst there I started to develop my illustration style.

At first I was influenced by the style, employed by the illustrators working on the film posters, a realistic style and I managed to get some book jackets in that style.

PR: Did you always have a strong sense of the work you wanted to do?

MT: Circa 1970 my friend Brian Grimwood introduced me to the iconic *Pushpin* studio of artists, Milton Glaser and Seymour Chwast. This exhibition was electrifying and I was very impressed by the work. The diverse richness of visual, inventive and individualistic artwork was very refreshing and had such an inspiring effect that my style and approach was beginning to take on a new look. During this time I produced illustrations for the *Observer* and the infant *Time Out*, working in a conceptual style.

I then decided to bring my humour into my work. I often drew caricatures of work colleagues, animals, situations and I caricatured people as they were presented to me, painting them in a realistic manner.

And there was my style!

One other influence was my interest in surrealism which appeared occasionally.

I am committed to what I believe in as an artist, I like

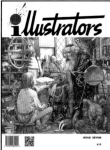

to view new work and to see how art is evolving within the media, so in a way the answer is yes, I have a strong sense of the work that I have done and of what I do, and also of where I want to go in the future.

This year in particular has offered me the opportunity to develop into the fine arts, which I have been working towards. This is a distance away from my illustrated and caricature work from the last forty years.

PR: Have you moved to creating art on the computer?
MT: No, I still like to work on board or paper in the traditional manner. I enjoy the craft of creating in this manner.

PR: Would you say it is easier to make illustration a career since you started?
MT: It was the beginning of a new era in illustration and in the '70's there was a greater abundance and opportunity with this type of work so making it easier to get started and to create your style.

PR: What advice would you give to people trying to make illustration their career?
MT: Believe in your work and in yourself. Talk to other illustrators and join the *Association of Illustrators*. Be open to changes in not only your style but in the media world of books and illustration. Agents are also a valuable source—find a suitable agent

PR: Do you think it necessary for people wanting to

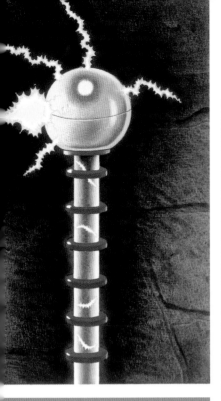

ABOVE: 'Snowgoose', one of a large number of pub signs that Terry was invited to design in the 1990s.
LEFT: Cockerel for a self-promotion, which led to a commission to produce a series of pub signs for *Vintage Inns*.
FAR LEFT: 'Farmer One', an example of one of the many signs Terry produced for *Vintage Inns*.
FAR LEFT TOP: 'Frankenstein's Monster' an ad for the *Electricity Board*'s share launch

ABOVE TOP: An Owl poster for *Essex Radio*, produced in the 1990s.
ABOVE: Stone-Age Essex girl for *Essex Radio*, 1990s.
RIGHT: 'Dovecote', another pub sign produced for *Vintage Inns* throughout much of the 1990s.
FACING PAGE: 'Bull' another of the poster designs created for *Essex Radio* in the 1990s.

work as professional illustrators to undertake a degree in illustration?

MT: I don't have a degree. It does however pay to go through college to have access to the facilities. To explore your own work and to see how you want to continue with the various mediums on offer. College offers such a wide range and with new technology it is better to experience all that the world of study in art can offer.

PR: Have you any projects you are particularly pleased with?

MT: Yes, very much so. In advertising there were quite a few: in particular, a series of big road side posters for *British Airways*; posters featuring caricatures of tennis players John McEnroe, Ilie Nastase, and Jimmy Connors for the *Queens Club Tennis Tournament* for a few years; a poster campaign for *Tiger Bitter*; posters for *Qantas Airlines*, and a series of posters for Ikea in Sweden and a series of posters and newspaper ads for the Electricity Board share offer in the early nineties and many more.

In children's books one of my favourites and my first picture book is 'The Selfish Crocodile', which turned into a best seller and, of course, the books I wrote and illustrated as well, notably my 'Captain Wag the Pirate Dog' series and 'The Rhino's Horns'.

The other field of illustration I have enjoyed is caricatures. As mentioned above there was the *Queens Club* series of posters, *TV Times, Sunday Telegraph, Punch, Observer Magazine* and the *Times* and others.

Apart from that, there were book jackets for a whole series of books featuring the likes of Mel Smith, Ian Botham, Spike Milligan, Michael Parkinson, Denis Norden and Frank Muir, Jimmy Edwards and Bob Monkhouse, to name a few.

It's funny how celebrities generally like their caricatures: Bob Monkhouse loved the one I did for his book and invited me over to his house to talk about my work, and Janet Street Porter contacted me to get the artwork of the caricature I did of her in *The Times*— and that was pretty extreme!

PR: Have you any projects that turned into a nightmare?

MT: Yes, in the not so distant past, which involved a large number of illustrations for a book that seriously went wrong, due to the clients not having been organised. Which resulted in delay after delay and then running out of time, so having to bring in another illustrator to work with me.

Overall in my career I have to say that I have been

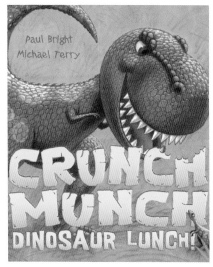

ABOVE: The cover to one of Mike's recent children's book commissions.
ABOVE TOP: A superb double page spread from 'Captain Wag Meets Pirate Ginger Tom', *Bloomsbury, 2007.*

very lucky and that I have had more success than failure.

PR: What would you like to work on for the future?

MT: Illustration is always close to my heart and I would like to continue with this. My artwork is such an immense part of my life and I will not be retiring.

I have recently produced more pieces on scraperboard for a fine art exhibition in Canterbury. This is an area that I am exploring. My fifty years of art has provided me with such a wonderful catalogue of events, of images of wild life that I have captured, which I now have time to do things with. I am also looking into sculpting. I have produced a few pieces before and would like to work more in different forms of sculpting

PR: If you were starting out all over again – would you still make illustration you career?

MT: Oh yes, without a doubt. It's such an overwhelming and awesome feeling to get a commission, such a thrill, so creatively rewarding and challenging.

I have been very fortunate in pursuing my career as a freelance illustrator. ●

● *For more of Mike Terry's amazing work check out:*
http://www.thepaintbrush.co.uk/

James E. McConnell (1903-1995) Original Art

Somewhere they Die
Paperback cover art 1958

The Hostile Hills
Paperback cover art 1960

Wagon Train
Magazine illustration 1977

Arouse and Beware
Paperback cover art 1958

 IllustrationArtGallery.com
The world's largest gallery of illustration paintings and comic strips
Tel: 020 8768 0022 (from outside UK+44 20 8768 0022) E: art@illustrationartgallery.com

Out There: Freya Hartas

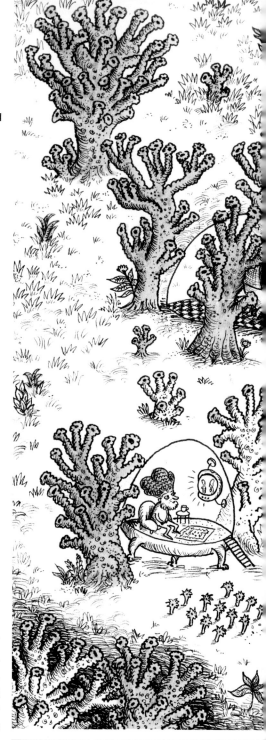

FREYA HARTAS GRADUATED from Falmouth College in 2014. Describing her years at Falmouth as "really enjoyable at one of the most idyllic places you could be an art student", she certainly hasn't let the grass grow under her feet. Her first commission came when she was still studying, and the resultant illustrations for the 'Dark Lord' series of books won the *Roald Dahl Funny Prize* in 2012. She was also among twelve illustrators who were awarded the *Lemniscaat Illustration Awards* for her picture book 'Little Kong'.

As Freya relates, "I've always loved drawing, my bunk bed as a child had drawings stuffed in every corner, even under the pillow, and I used to stay up all night drawing mice... I was quite obsessed with them for some

ABOVE: A scene from Freya's 'Glasshouses', in which a spaceman crash lands on a planet where everything, including the people, is covered with a bright yellow fungus.

LEFT: 'Three Headed Beasts', Freya's line work is achieved with a dip pen—the colour in this example was then added digitally after scanning her artwork..

FAR LEFT: A vignette from 'Millie's Toys', drawn in pencil with washes of watercolour added.

FAR LEFT TOP: 'Creature', Freya's line work has a deliciously retro feel about it.

RIGHT: 'Millie's Toys'. One of
a series of illustrations depicting
the adventures of a little girl
and her toys.
BELOW: 'Witches' from the award
winning 'The Dark Lord', written
by Jamie Thomson and published
by *Orchard Books*.
BOTTOM: Another of Freya's
award winners—'Little Kong',
published by *Lemniscaat* 2015.

reason. I don't think there was ever a point when I decided I wanted to be an illustrator, it just sort of happened".

Although both her father, Leo Hartas and grandfather, John Vernon Lord (see *illustrators* issue 7), are illustrators, Freya is far from sanguine about the prospects of making it as a full-time illustrator but, with the talent, drive and application she has already displayed, one can't help but think that she is going to succeed.

For more of Freya's work and a chance to buy some of her hand-made art check these links:

Her website:

http://freyahartas.co.uk

Her blog:

http://freyahartas.tumblr.com

Her Etsy shop:

http://www.etsy.com/uk/shop/FreyaHartasShop

James E. McConnell (1903-1995) Original Art

The Charge of the Light Brigade
Magazine illustration 1967

Zulu War Dance
Magazine illustration 1974

The Bookshelf

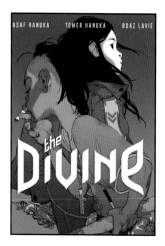

Becoming A Successful Illustrator
By Jo Davies & Derek Brazell
Paperback 192 pages
Fairchild Books £21.59/ $40.80
(also available in the UK as
a Kindle edition £16.19)

ILLUSTRATION AS A PROFESSION has witnessed seismic changes over the last decade. It's easy for many established practitioners of the craft to bemoan the erosion of fees and the increasingly uncertain environment that contractions in traditional sources of employment have created.

That is why this book by Jo Davies and Derek Brazell is so refreshing—for anyone contemplating a career in illustration it's an absolute must read and, for even the casual enthusiast of illustration, there is a lot of insight to be gleaned from the contents of this delightful book.

The tone of the book is upbeat, whilst acknowledging the challenges and demands placed upon illustrators. The book is broken down into sections such as folio presentation, understanding your commissioners, self-promotion, invoicing and book keeping. In essence, the skill sets which need to be adhered to for the pursuit of a career in illustration, with spotlights being shed on a selection of successful practitioners who share their experiences and offer advice.

Definitely a book which should be read and absorbed by all aspiring illustrators and a must for every college library.

The Divine
Written by Boas Lavie
Illustrated by Asaf
and Tomer Hanuka
Paperback 160 pages
First Second £14.99/ $15.47

ASAF AND TOMER HANUKA are twins, who have managed to establish careers as successful illustrators and while their work doesn't exactly mirror each other, it does spring from the same shared passions of their formative years.

As a consequence, they will often collaborate on projects together and 'The Divine' is just such a project. Celebrated screenwriter Boaz Lavie's story of ex-army buddies, Mark and Jason, navigating their way through the war-torn landscape of 'Quanlom' to fulfil a well-paid but perilous mining contract makes for a very unsettling read. There is the all too familiar iconography of AK 47s and child soldiers, which Lavie counterpoints with a surreal and hallucinogenic juxtaposition of gods, demons and creatures beyond our ken.

The Hanuka brothers' treatment of Lavie's script makes for a thoroughly gripping read, with Asaf's pencils complimented by Tomer's inking and sublime colouring, making this story their most impressive collaboration to date.

For fans of Asaf and Tomer Hanuka's work, as well as lovers of exceptional graphic novels, this is an essential addition to the library.

Making It
Produced and Directed by Tony Moorman
Featuring Andrew Bawidamann,
Brian Ewing and Eric Fortune
Running time 1 hour and 28 minutes
www.makingitpictures.com $9.99

THIS DOCUMENTARY IS one of the most important examinations of what is required to "make it" as an illustrator, in what is a far from benign environment.

Whilst considering just what defines "making it", the film looks at the lives of three illustrators at the top of their game. Eric Fortune, Brian Ewing and Andrew Bawidamann are all artists, whose work has garnered awards and acclaim. But as the camera pries beneath the veneer of success, the artists that it reveals are far from basking in the comfort and certainty that the casual observer and many of their fans and followers might surmise.

For many putative artists, the concept of "making it" is the ability to fund oneself entirely from one's own creativity. This is what all the protagonists in this film have achieved, but it is the singularity and obsessive focus required to get there that many viewers may find disconcerting.

While this film is definitely not devoted to technique and procedure (there is plenty of that out in YouTube land already), this documentary does present a compelling look at the sheer discipline and drive required to carve out a career as an illustrator in the 21st century. Required viewing for all aspirant illustrators.

● ***illustrators*** is also available in the USA from **budplant.com**

ALPINE ANGST: Gustav Doré's vertigo-inducing depiction of Edmund Whymper's disasterous descent of the Matterhorn on 14th July 1865. The production of the artwork created considerable unease for Whymper, who was in the depths of survivor's guilt and mourning the loss of his companions. Dore had been so exorcised by reading of the disaster that he produced several drawings based on Whymper's account. Whymper, who was already under close scrutiny for the circumstances which had led to the loss of life of a party that included the aristocratic, Lord Francis Douglas, was further discomforted by requests from Dore's publisher for as much additional detail as could be furnished. The images of his companions sliding to their doom were to haunt Whymper until the end of his days.

Hi Peter, thanks so much for the magazine—it all looks well up to standard. The stand-out for me is John Haslam—his stuff is great and he's a lovely guy.

Best Wishes,
—**Mick Brownfield**

Dear Peter, Copies of *illustrators* 8 arrived today. All I can say is Wow! Actually, I can say more. The publication is beautiful and I have never had my text so beautifully presented. Surely, this will become a collector's edition!

Certainly I will sign and forward four copies to you. I hope to do this on Wednesday (tied up all day tomorrow).

Thank you for including me in this wonderful project.

Best wishes,
—**David Stuart Davies**

To say we were flattered by David's email would be something of an understatement. David is an award winning playwright, editor and writer and one of the leading authorities on Sherlock Holmes.

Peter—I have received the copies of Issue 8 and would like to say a sincere "thank you" for publishing such a wonderful article!

I am very flattered and honoured to be profiled in *illustrators*. The reproduction quality of all of the images is outstanding.

I only wish Bryn were still with us so I could thank him, as well, for all of his work on the piece.

Many thanks,
—*Bart Forbes*

A sentiment that we wholeheartedly echo Bart. Bryn contributed so much to illustrators and he will be sorely missed by all of us.

We were honoured to receive the following from the doyen of science fiction cover art Bruce Pennington—

Dear Peter, Thanks very much for the sample copy of *illustrators* issue 9, which reached me in excellent condition. I look forward to getting any comments from readers in due course.

It's a really high quality production.

With much gratitude and Best Wishes,
—**Bruce Pennington**

Dear Peter, Many thanks for the copies of *illustrators* 9. Bruce (Pennington)'s article looks brilliant and reads really well. I've put a mention of it on his website.

Best wishes and keep up the good work!
—**Nigel Suckling**

With almost 100 interviews and articles published over the last 8 years, I'd say this one will be my most treasured.

A wonderfully written 25 page interview covering my work and touching on the whys, hows and everything in between *proud*
—**Joanna Henley aka Miss Led**

We were both amazed and delighted by Miss Led's recent Facebook posting— thank you Jo!

First off, congratulations on a splendid edition of *illustrators*. Apart from that excellent piece on Parker, I loved the art of Miss Led, who is completely new to me, and it was great to see so much of Bruce Pennington's work, which I have always admired and his alien image made a most arresting cover. Your obituary on Bryn was a wonderful warm evocation of the man; your liking and admiration for him and his talents shone through. I now look forward to the next issue and the Nicolle!

Best Wishes,
—**David Ashford**

I loved this issue so much. Pennington was the artist of my awakening interest in SF. His interpretation of the Bradbury covers shows he might not have read the books but who cares!!! And Miss Led's work is gorgeous - never heard of

her before!

Best wishes,
—**Norman Boyd**

I got a very nice feature/write up in *illustrators* magazine in issue #9! Thank you Peter Richardson - this is a must have magazine for illustrators

Thank You!
—**Will Terry**

The pleasure is all ours Will!

Coming Soon!

The ultimate insight into the Spanish artists whose work transformed comics across Europe and the US. The influence of the *SI Studios* and it's visionary founder Josep Toutain has often been referred to but never before has the full story been told. In an *illustrators special*, insider, Diego Cordoba reveals the men who added their own particular blend of romance and horror to comics in general and Warren publishing in particular. Featuring the work of Enric, Sanjulian, 'Pepe' Gonzalez, Luis Garcia, Esteban Maroto and Jordi Bernet—this issue is one to watch out for.

● **Please send your comments to the editor, Peter Richardson, at Illustrators. The Book Palace. Jubilee House. Bedwardine Road. Crystal Palace. LONDON. SE19 3AP, or email him at** *p-r@dircon.co.uk*